Mysterious Healing

Brian Innes

RSVP

RAINTREE
STECK-VAUGHN
P U B L I S H E R S
A Steck-Vaughn Company

Austin, Texas

www.steck-vaughn.com

Developed by Brown Partworks
Editor: Lindsey Lowe
Designer: Joan Curtis
Picture Researcher: Brigitte Arora

Raintree Steck-Vaughn Publishers Staff
Project Manager: Joyce Spicer
Editor: Pam Wells

Library of Congress Cataloging-in-Publication Data
Innes, Brian.
    Mysterious healing/by Brian Innes.
        p.   cm.—(Unsolved mysteries)
    Includes bibliographical references and index.
    Summary: Describes reported instances of psychic healing and offers some
possible explanations of these phenomena.
    ISBN 0-8172-5489-7 (Hardcover)
    ISBN 0-8172-5851-5 (Softcover)
    1. Spiritual healing—Juvenile literature. 2. Supernatural—Juvenile literature.
[1. Mental healing.] I. Title. II. Series: Innes, Brian. Unsolved mysteries.
BT732.5.I55   1999
615.8.52—dc21   98-38216
                                                                  CIP
                                                                  AC
Printed and bound in the United States
1 2 3 4 5 6 7 8 9 0   WZ   02 01 00 99 98

Acknowledgments

Cover: Michel Tcherevkoff/The Image Bank;
Page 5: Adrian Arbib/Corbis; **Page 6:** Cyril
Permutt/Society for Psychical Research/Mary Evans
Picture Library; **Page 7:** Dr. Elmar R. Gruber/Fortean
Picture Library; **Page 9:** Guy Lyon Playfair/Mary
Evans Picture Library; **Page 11:** Edgar Cayce
Foundation; **Page 13:** Hulton-Deutsch Collection/
Corbis; **Page 14:** Klaus Aarsleff/Fortean Picture
Library; **Page 15:** Dr. Elmar R. Gruber/Fortean
Picture Library; **Page 17:** Nik Wheeler/Corbis;
Page 18: Hodder & Stoughton Publishers; **Page 19:**
Mary Evans Picture Library; **Page 20:** Yan Arthus-
Bertrand/Corbis; **Page 21:** Sue Cunningham/SCP;
Page 22: Guy Lyon Playfair/Mary Evans Picture
Library; **Page 24:** Richard Gardner/Rex Features;
Page 25: Dr. Elmar R. Gruber/Fortean Picture
Library; **Page 27:** Michael S. Yamashita/Corbis;
Page 28: Keren Su/Corbis; **Page 29:** Wolfgang
Kaehler/Corbis; **Page 30:** Guy Lyon Playfair/Fortean
Picture Library; **Page 31:** Morton Beebe-S.F./Corbis;
Page 33: Harnzeh Carr/Images Colour Library;
Page 34: Corbis-Bettmann; **Page 35:** Charles Walker
Collection/Images Colour Library; **Page 36:** Mary
Evans Picture Library; **Page 37:** Dr. Elmar R.
Gruber/Fortean Picture Library; **Page 39:** Images
Colour Library; **Page 41:** Lowell Georgia/Corbis;
Page 42: Richard T. Nowitz/Corbis; **Page 44:** Larry
Mulvehill/Science Photo Library; **Page 45:** Dr. P.
Marazzi/Science Photo Library; **Page 46:** Mirror
Syndication International.

Contents

A Healing Touch

There have been huge advances in medical science over the centuries. However, scientists still cannot explain the power of the healing touch.

A man using his powers of psychic healing to cure a patient in Namibia, in southwest Africa, (opposite).

At the age of 19, Rose Gladden discovered that she had a special gift: "I had gone into a shop in London, called Dyers & Chapman, and found Mr. Chapman . . . lying under the counter. I asked him what was wrong, and he said, 'I'm in terrible pain. I have an ulcer [a sore].' Now, I didn't know where that ulcer was. All I thought was, 'I wish I could help him,' and I heard a voice say, 'You can. Put your hand there.'"

MYSTERIOUS HAND

Then, Gladden said, a little star appeared, just as if it had fallen out of the night sky. It floated over Chapman's left shoulder and then hovered over the top half of his stomach. Chapman said this was where the ulcer was.

Rose Gladden told what happened, "As I put my hand there I felt, but never saw, another hand come over mine and hold it steady. I felt my hand being filled with . . . heat. I couldn't move it away. . . . After a while, my hand was pulled . . . to his side, and then away from his body. Then, Mr. Chapman said, 'Your fingers felt as if they were holding the pain and, as you took your hand across, the pain went with it.'"

4

In the past such healing skills were said to be "miracles."

MIRACLE CURE

In the past such healing skills were said to be "miracles." But hundreds of seemingly ordinary people in the 20th century have discovered that they also have the power to heal—by touch alone.

This power is not the same as the skills that are used by masseurs or osteopaths, who also use their hands to help people. A masseur is someone who rubs the muscles to ease stiffness in the body. An osteopath is someone who gently moves the bones in the body, often without the use of surgery. An osteopath tries to put back any bone or joint that might have slipped out of place and so be causing pain.

Rose Gladden healing a man in 1978. This photograph was taken at a public exhibition.

The healer, however, merely puts his or her hands gently on the patient. He or she thinks hard about making a healing power "flow" from their hands into the patient's body. Some patients may feel heat where they are touched. Others say they feel "something like an electric shock," or see bright colors.

THINKING AWAY THE PAIN

By 1980 Englishman Matthew Manning had become well-known as a psychic healer. He was then just 24 years old. As a teenager Manning had already shown that he had all kinds of mysterious powers. Then, in 1977, he decided to devote his life to healing.

Manning says that the healing does not come from him. He claims that it passes through him. "I am merely a channel," he says. The successful healer should "see" what he or she wants to happen.

Manning has described how he cures a patient of back pain: "I imagine the pain symbolized [represented] by a large red area. In my imagination I see the spine surrounded with red. I then just imagine that I have an enormous sponge. I imagine that I am pushing the sponge into the body, and I imagine the sponge is absorbing all the redness. And, when the sponge is completely red, I just imagine I am . . . squeezing the sponge. And I watch the pain and the redness fall away, until the sponge is completely clean. Then I go back to the spine, mopping up the pain until it has completely disappeared."

Matthew Manning at a show of his healing skills in Baden-Baden, Germany, in the late 1970s.

PINS AND NEEDLES

While healing a patient, Manning often feels heat and tingling, or a feeling of pins and needles. So do many of his patients. After a visit to Manning, one patient said, "When he placed his hands on my head, I felt a slight tremble . . . inside my head. At the moment he touched the base of my neck, I felt as though something was being drawn from my spine."

DENTIST WITH A MISSION

One of the most amazing stories involving healing by touch is that of the "psychic dentist" William Fuller.

Fuller trained in business studies and science before becoming a minister in the Baptist Church. After ten years he began to practice as a healer. Bryce Bond, an American writer, described the simple way that Fuller heals: "He gently smacks the person on both cheeks at the same time."

Matthew Manning went to one of Fuller's healing sessions in New York in 1979. He reported: "One woman had, at the back of her jaw, a very decayed [rotten] tooth. . . . I saw it fill with something white. . . . When finished, she had a new white tooth. . . . I saw this happen."

She was amazed when . . . her silver-colored metal fillings changed into gold.

SEEING IS BELIEVING

Most doctors and dentists refused to believe that Fuller could really do these things. However, some scientists from the National Aeronautics and Space Administration (NASA) received dental healing from Fuller. They met him at a public show of his skills in Miami, Florida.

A number of doctors also went to a 1979 meeting at Wagner College, in New York City. One of these doctors was Audrey Kargere from Stockholm, Sweden. She was amazed when several of her silver-colored metal fillings changed into gold. Another doctor, Peter Williams, was at the meeting. He was delighted but puzzled when his rotten tooth became a "bright, shiny gold" following treatment by Fuller.

CUTTING NEW TEETH

One 66-year-old woman is said to have gone to Fuller for help. She had lost all her own teeth. She told Fuller that her dentures, or false teeth, were too loose. The next day she called him to complain that they were too tight. The following day she called again. She said that now the plates did not fit at all. Then, 24 hours later, she called once more. "I know why my plates don't fit," she said. "I'm cutting new teeth like a baby." Within 17 days, it was claimed, she had 32 new teeth!

William Fuller examining a patient at a public meeting in 1985. Fuller's amazing powers as a psychic dentist could not be explained by scientists.

Other Types of Healing

Some healers seem to be able to cure people just by touching them. Others use different methods.

The laying on of hands is just one of the many types of psychic or mysterious healing. Another kind is known as "distant healing." With this method it is not even necessary for the healer to be anywhere near the patient.

One well-known person who practiced distant healing was Edgar Cayce. He was born on a small farm in Hopkinsville, Kentucky, in 1877. At age 16 he was badly hurt when he was struck in the back by a baseball. He was told to stay in bed. One day he suddenly told his mother to cover his back with a hot poultice, which is a type of healing ointment spread on a bandage. In the morning his pain had gone.

Soon afterward, Cayce had a very bad throat infection. It seemed likely that he would lose his voice forever. A hypnotist named Al Layne helped him to go into a sleeplike state. When he woke up, he was cured!

TREATING THE SICK

As an adult, Edgar Cayce decided to devote his life to treating the sick. Sometimes his patients visited him at his home. More often, however, he used his powers of distant healing.

Edgar Cayce (opposite) was a psychic. He spent his life healing people. He was also well-known for predicting what would happen in the future.

Somehow . . . he was able to examine the distant patient while he was in a sleeplike state.

In both cases Cayce would lie down on a couch. With cases of distant healing, one of his helpers—often his wife—would then give him the name and address of a patient. Somehow, Cayce claimed, he was able to examine the distant patient while he was in a sleeplike state. He would then describe what treatment should be used. Sometimes he suggested surgery or medicine. At other times he described unusual cures with herbs. In some cases he said the patient needed to do nothing more than exercise. When he died in 1945, Cayce had successfully treated over 15,000 people.

Everyone was amazed—his doctors had not expected the man to live much longer.

GET-WELL MESSAGE

Another famous healer was Englishman Harry Edwards. He began his work almost by accident. He was more than 40 years old when he heard that a friend of someone he knew was dying. Edwards sat quietly and thought hard about the person.

Pictures came into Edwards's mind. He "saw" a row of hospital beds. The bed next to the last one in the row seemed to be particularly important. Still thinking hard, Edwards sent the man a telepathic "get-well" message. Telepathy is when thoughts or messages are sent from one person's mind to someone else's. It seems to have no scientific explanation.

When Edwards talked to his friend, he found that his imagined picture of the hospital was exactly what

This woman was once unable to walk. Here, the crowd watches in amazement as healer Harry Edwards helps her to walk again during his show at London's Royal Festival Hall in 1951.

it really looked like. The patient soon reported that he was feeling better and shortly afterward he went back to work. Everyone was amazed—his doctors had not expected the man to live much longer.

ANOTHER PATIENT

Not long after this event a woman went to see Edwards in London. She was very worried and needed to talk to someone. She told him that her husband was dying of cancer. He had been sent home from the hospital because the doctors had said there was nothing more they could do to help him. Edwards also felt that there was little he could do. However, he decided to try distant healing. Once again he sent a telepathic get-well message.

ANOTHER SUCCESS

Because she didn't want to get his hopes up, the woman did not tell her husband about her visit to Edwards. Two days later she went to see him again. She told him that her husband seemed to be better. In fact, the man lived for another 20 years—never knowing that Edwards had played any part in his recovery. After this experience Edwards decided to take up healing full-time.

13

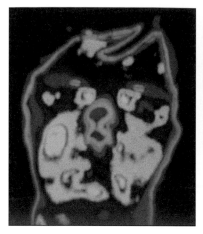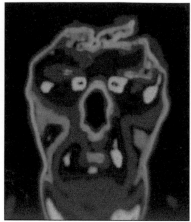

Doctors and scientists often take special pictures of patients to show how much heat is being given off by different parts of the body. The pictures are called thermograms. The thermograms above show the face of a patient before and after psychic healing treatment. The face is quite swollen in the picture on the left, and the yellow areas show heat coming off the cheeks. Following healing, right, the patient's temperature has gone down. This loss of heat energy, either from the patient or the healer, is common during psychic healing.

Edwards's first patient was a young girl who was suffering from a lung disease. In this case, Edwards decided to use the healing powers of his hands. When he placed his hands on the girl's head, he felt as he had never felt before. He said his whole body seemed to be filled with a powerful energy. He said heat flowed down his arms and out through his hands into the patient. Afterward, he found himself telling the girl's mother that her daughter would get well and be out of bed in three days. This proved to be the case. At her next medical checkup, the doctors said she appeared to be completely cured.

Until his death in 1976, Edwards practiced "hands on" healing on thousands of patients. He became so famous that on one occasion 8,000 people went to see him at the Albert Hall in London. They went in order to be treated, or just to watch him in action.

AMAZING LIGHT CURES

There are other mysterious healing methods that do not use the laying on of hands or distant healing. Scientists are equally puzzled by them.

One of these methods is called color therapy, or color healing. In color therapy, a colored light is shone on the part of the body that needs to have treatment. For example, red light is often used to treat skin problems. Another way of using colored light is colorpuncture. This is something like the ancient Chinese healing method called acupuncture. In acupuncture, needles are pushed into the skin at special places. The needles are said to release the body's natural healing powers. However, with color therapy or colorpuncture the healer does not put needles into the skin. Instead a thin beam of bright light is shone directly onto particular areas of the patient's body.

This woman is being treated with a colored light therapy called colorpuncture. This was developed in Germany by Peter Mandel.

A POSSIBLE EXPLANATION?

It has been suggested that light may cause some type of activity in the hypothalamus. This is a part of the brain that helps to control many of the body's everyday functions.

Although scientists have not been able to come up with an explanation for psychic healing, it seems that there may be some scientific reason for the success of light therapy.

15

Psychic Surgery

If Lyall Watson had not seen it for himself, he would not have believed in psychic surgery. But what did he see?

A psychic surgeon and his assistants healing a patient in the Philippines (opposite).

English scientist and writer Lyall Watson first became famous in 1973 when he wrote his book *Supernature*. In this book he described all sorts of different psychic events. Three years later, in another book called *The Romeo Error*, Watson described how he had watched various healers at work in the Philippines.

The Philippines are a group of islands off the southeast coast of Asia, and Watson had visited these islands on three separate occasions. Over a period of eight months, he had watched over 1,000 operations that were carried out by 22 different healers. Because of the way in which they work, these healers are usually known as "psychic surgeons."

SEEING IS BELIEVING

One of the operations watched by Watson was carried out on a woman who was complaining of stomach pains. She lay down on a wooden table. She remained fully dressed. A small part of her stomach was then uncovered and a large towel was put over her skirt to protect it. Watson checked the towel carefully to make sure that there was nothing hidden in it.

"I rub my hand over her skin. It is hot, but there is nothing on it, not a mark of any kind."

LYALL WATSON

Scientist Lyall Watson. He had watched some 1,000 operations done by psychic healers in the Philippines. In the 1970s he wrote about them in his books Supernature *and* The Romeo Error.

The "surgeon" was dressed in cotton trousers and a short-sleeved shirt. He seemed to murmur a few words. Watson handed him a wad of cotton and a bowl of water filled from the tap. The healer used these to wash the woman's skin. Then he seemed to push his hands into her stomach. The woman was not in any pain, and the healer had not cut her skin in any way. Watson described what happened next: "He is now working just to the right of her navel, and suddenly there is a red color. It could be blood."

REMOVING THE PROBLEM

Suddenly a lump began to appear between two of the fingers on the healer's hand. In seconds it was about the size of a tennis ball. An assistant reached forward and lifted the ball clear of the woman's body. When the skin of the patient's stomach was wiped clean, Watson was amazed to see that there was no sign of a wound. He noted down what he was seeing: "I rub my hand over her skin. It is hot, but there is nothing on it, not a mark of any kind." The woman slowly got up and walked away.

SOUTH AMERICAN CURES

There are hundreds of "psychic surgeons" in the Philippines. People from all over the world have gone there hoping to be healed. The first man known to practice this type of healing was Eleuterio Terte. He was born in 1905 in St. Fabian, on the island of Luzon. Terte's father was a leading member of a psychic group called the "Spiritists," who believed in something known as Spiritism.

The idea of Spiritism began in Brazil in the 1860s. Denizard Rivail, known as "Allen Kardec," was a French doctor. He had written a book about his belief in many otherworldly, or spiritual, powers.

Denizard Rivail, or Allen Kardec, the 19th-century doctor. His book led to the development of Spiritism in Brazil.

A Brazilian nobleman had read this book and was fascinated by Kardec's ideas. The nobleman took a copy of the book from France to Rio de Janeiro, his hometown in Brazil. There a new religion sprang up. This was called Spiritism. It was based on Allen Kardec's ideas of spiritualism, but also included ideas from the Christian and traditional African religions. The new religion combined belief in many gods with the worship of ancient ancestors. Spiritism is now mainly practiced in Haiti in the West Indies.

SPIRITISM SPREADS

Today there are more than 3,000 Spiritist chapels in Brazil alone. Believers concentrate on curing the body, so that the mind can work properly. This is mainly done by the laying on of hands. There are three major Spiritist hospitals in Brazil. From Brazil the practice spread to the Philippines.

A view of Rio de Janeiro from one of the mountain peaks surrounding Guanabara Bay. Rio de Janeiro is home to thousands of Spiritist believers.

This woman is healing people using laying on of hands. She is taking part in a healing ceremony in Salvador, Bahia State, Brazil.

SPIRITUAL BEINGS

Spiritism found many followers in the Philippines, particularly on the island of Luzon, where Eleuterio Terte was born. One day Terte became seriously ill. He said that while he was sick with a fever he was visited by two spiritual beings. They said he would recover, but only if he agreed to become a healer.

For many years Terte treated the sick simply by touching them with his hands. But then World War II broke out in 1939. When the Japanese invaded the Philippines in December 1941, Terte had to go and fight. At the end of the war, in 1945, he became sick once more. Again, Terte said, he was visited by the beings. They told him he must become a surgeon. To his surprise, he found that he could operate using just his bare hands. Gradually he became famous for this.

21

During the 1950s Terte was visited by people from all over the world. Then, in 1966, he set up a group that was named the "Christian Spiritists of the Philippines."

Today this group has a membership of more than 50,000 people. Many of them practice as healers. There are still more than 20 healers still alive who were trained by Eleuterio Terte himself.

BRAZIL'S "MIRACLE DOCTOR"

In Brazil the most famous psychic surgeon was José Pedro de Freitas. He was known to the people as "Ze Arigo." He claimed that he was guided in his healing by a Dr. Fritz, a German doctor, long dead, whom he had never met.

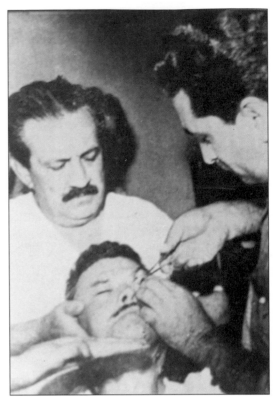

Ze Arigo applying a piece of cotton wadding to a patient's eye. Ze Arigo performed many potentially dangerous operations in the 1960s.

Ze Arigo was said to have treated as many as 300 patients every day. He did this for 20 years. It is claimed that he could stop the flow of blood simply by telling it to stop. However, the Brazilian Medical Association and the Catholic Church eventually took legal action against Ze Arigo. They said he should not be operating on people because he was not a qualified medical doctor. He was put in jail twice, in 1958 and 1964. But thousands of people told the courts that they had been cured by him. When he left prison, he continued his work. He would not be put off by the threat of going to jail.

In 1966 Andrija Puharich, an American who was interested in psychic happenings, took a team of doctors to Brazil to speak to Ze Arigo. After their visit Puharich said he was sure that Ze Arigo had special healing powers that could not be explained. Other scientists were interested in his story. Unfortunately, however, Ze Arigo died in an automobile accident on January 11, 1971. His powers remain a mystery.

PROOF OF TRICKERY

Doctors and scientists who use generally recognized medical methods say that "psychic surgery" is just trickery. They have good reason to believe this. Some scientists have been able to look at samples of material that is claimed to have been removed from patients. Sometimes these samples have been found to be different parts of chickens or pigs. "Kidney stones" have turned out to be simple pebbles.

It is claimed that he could stop the flow of blood simply by telling it to stop.

The blood from some operations has also been examined. Much of it was found to be pigs' blood. In some cases scientists could not find out what it was. Other people discovered that some "surgeons" hid little plastic bags of blood in the palm of the hand. Their hands did not actually enter the body of

23

This is James Randi who, over the years, has revealed that many so-called psychic happenings are nothing but tricks.

the patient. Instead, they had just folded their knuckles under their palms into a tight fist. Then they had pushed against the body where the fat was thickest. But it looked as if they had pushed their fingers into the flesh of their patients.

In 1979 a program about a couple called David and Helen Elizalde appeared on television in Britain. The couple lived in Australia, but David was actually from the Philippines. He and his wife were filmed carrying out an operation in England. Afterward, blood from the operation was checked by scientists. It was found to be pigs' blood.

A former stage magician called James Randi has always laughed at "psychic" events. In the television program he successfully copied the Elizaldes' "operation" using magicians' trickery.

PROOF OF A CURE

The mystery, however, remains. Hundreds of people are sure that they have been cured by this type of psychic surgery. One of these is Englishwoman Anne Dooley. In 1982 she described an operation that had been carried out on her 16 years earlier.

In 1946, when she was only 34, Dooley's doctors told her that she had a serious lung condition. This could not be operated on. In 1959 a doctor told her that she would have to take medicine for the rest of her life. In 1966 she asked Brazilian Lourival de Freitas for help. Although he used slightly more conventional methods than other psychic surgeons, he did not use medicines or modern equipment.

Lourival made a tiny cut under Dooley's right shoulder blade. Later Dooley said she felt him "grip and squeeze my flesh. Next I found myself being handed . . . what looked like . . . blood about the size of a coin." She said that she had felt "very little pain," and "there was no bleeding."

This is Allen Kardec's grave in Paris, France. Most scientists do not believe that psychic healing really works. However, thousands of people from all over the world journey to Paris each year to put flowers on Kardec's grave. They are people who claim to have been cured by psychic healers. Surely they can't all have been mistaken?

STILL GOING STRONG

Sixteen years later, Anne Dooley was still in good health and was not having to take any medicines. Her doctors were amazed. They had no explanation for it. They said that the best they could have done for her was to keep her going for as long as possible. They were sure that she would not have lived another 16 years. Dooley also said, "I myself don't think I would be here if I hadn't volunteered for psychic surgery."

Healing in the East

There are many types of healing in the East. Most are concerned with releasing what is called the life force.

This is the door of a house in the South Korean village of Suwon (opposite). The circles painted on the door represent the combined life forces of yin (blue) and yang (orange).

In recent years many people in the Western world, such as the United States and Europe, have started to use healing methods from the East—China, Japan, and India.

Traditional Chinese and Japanese healers treat both the mind and the body at the same time. Chinese and Japanese healing shares one basic belief. This is *chi* (sometimes spelled *qi* or *ki*). According to Chinese tradition, chi was the single cell from which the entire universe grew. It is claimed that this cell broke into two halves. These became the life forces of *yin* and *yang*.

YIN AND YANG

According to Far Eastern beliefs, everything in the universe is made up of the forces of yin and yang. Yang is said to be light, the Sun, an active, dry force. Yin is dark, the Earth, a peaceful, wet force. Yang enters the human body, flowing downward from above. Yin flows upward from the Earth. For a person to be in good health, both life forces must be present in the body.

Chi is the life force. It is air and breath. It is energy that flows through the human body and throughout the universe. It passes through the

26

According to Far Eastern beliefs, everything in the universe is made up of the forces of yin and yang.

body along paths that are called "meridians." There are said to be 12 meridians that lead from the lungs to all parts of the body. In addition, chi is said to flow through eight paths in the brain.

CONTROLLING THE CHI

If the chi is not flowing properly through the body, either because there is too much or too little of it, then the flow must be changed. There are many different points along the 12 meridians where this can be carried out. Sharp needles are gently stuck into the skin at these points. This controls and corrects the flow of chi. All kinds

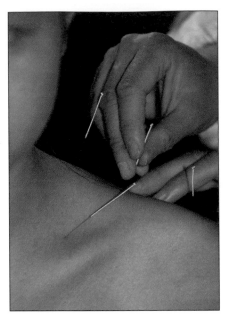

A patient receiving acupuncture in Peking. The acupuncture needles are inserted by an expert at specific points in the body.

of diseases of the mind and body can be treated in this way. This type of healing is called acupuncture.

Another Eastern healing method something like acupuncture is acupressure. Instead of using needles, the thumb and fingers are pressed firmly on each of the acupuncture points of the body noted by the Chinese. Another form of acupressure, Shiatsu, was developed in Japan. People who practice it use their fingers, thumbs, forearms, elbows, or knees—some even walk on the patient!

MARTIAL ARTS

The ancient martial arts of China and Japan also have a healing, spiritual side. Martial arts are any of the sports involving fighting skills—such as judo and karate—that were developed in Eastern countries.

Although the Japanese martial art of aikido also involves fighting skills, it is usually practiced as a self-defense system. Aikido puts as much emphasis on training the mind and spirit as it does on training the body. An example is the aikido exercise called "the unbendable arm." The arm is held out straight in front of the body. Someone else is then asked to bend it. This is easy to do if the arm is held out stiffly. However, the secret is to think of the stretched arm as a rubber hose through which the body's energy is flowing out. It then becomes much more difficult for the other person to bend the arm.

TAPPING INTO THE CHI

T'ai Chi is another form of Chinese martial art now popular in the West. It involves both attack and defense skills and can be carried out with or without weapons. In its simplest form, T'ai Chi is a series of

People practicing T'ai Chi. In many Eastern countries, people practice T'ai Chi together every morning. This picture was taken next to the outer wall of the Forbidden City in Beijing, China.

relaxation exercises. However, the belief is that when a person does these exercises correctly, he or she is able to "tap into" the chi flowing through the universe. This is said to make a person strong and healthy in both mind and body.

Reiki healing at the 1997 Festival of Mind Body Spirit, in London.

A CLEAR MIND

Western healers have also begun to use reiki. This is a form of healing that began in Japan in the late 19th century. It was first used by Dr. Miako Usui. Reiki is something like the laying on of hands.

Dr. Usui spent 21 years studying various forms of healing in Kyoto, Japan. This was followed by 21 days alone on a mountain. While he was there, he did not eat anything. He tried to clear his mind of the problems and worries of everyday life. Following this, Dr. Usui found that he had special healing powers. He met a girl suffering from toothache. He put his hands on her jaw and after a few minutes, the girl's toothache was gone.

Dr. Usui spent many years healing people. He was guided by his five simple rules of Reiki:

Just for today, I will let go of anger.
Just for today, I will let go of worry.
Today, I will count my many blessings.
Today, I will do my work honestly.
Today, I will be kind to every living creature.

INDIAN HEALING

Hindu teachers believe in a life energy something like chi. They call it *prana*. From this comes what is called *pranayama*, which is the control of breathing. It is an important part of yoga. It is claimed that sick people do not have enough prana.

One of the oldest healing methods is the Hindu practice of *ayurveda*. Like other Eastern healing, ayurveda treats the patient's mind and body. The aim is to prevent illnesses. Ayurveda involves yoga, exercises, advice on personal cleanliness, and special diets. However, if a cure is needed for a condition that is already known to exist, then ayurveda is often combined with scientific medicine.

Practicing yoga at sunrise in California. Yoga, involves the control of breathing, or pranayama, ed in India and is now practiced worldwide.

PERSONAL TREATMENT

When an ayurvedic doctor wants to find out what is wrong with a patient, he or she first asks various questions. The answers help the doctor to find out what kind of person the patient is. This is a very important part of ayurveda. Since everyone is different, people need to be given different treatments.

The patient's pulse, or heartbeat, is then taken. From this, ayurvedic doctors claim they can find any problems that need to be cured. To make the person well again, the healer must correct the flow of life forces in the body—this is something like the release of a person's chi in acupuncture.

31

"Seeing" Sickness

Can you tell what is wrong with people just by looking at them? Some healers claim they can. But how do they do it?

If we are sick, the doctor tries to find out what is wrong with us. This process is called diagnosis. The doctor measures body temperature with an instrument called a thermometer. Our pulse—the speed and strength at which the heart is beating—is taken. The doctor listens to the heart and lungs using a stethoscope, and looks for spots on the skin. Healers sometimes do the same things, but they also claim to be able to see things that the doctor cannot.

GUIDING LIGHT

When healer Rose Gladden first treated a sick person, she said a speck of light showed her where to lay her hands. In later years she told how she sometimes "saw" lines and dots of silvery light on people's bodies. Strangely, these were often in places far from where her patients said they had a pain. However, Gladden found that placing her hands on the dots of light seemed to cure the person.

At other times, Gladden said, she could see a person's "aura." Healers believe that an aura is a kind of misty glow of many colors. Certain people say that they can see an aura surrounding

People have believed in auras for centuries. This painting (opposite) is one artist's idea of what an aura might look like.

Healers believe that an aura is a kind of misty glow of many colors.

every human body, as well as animals, plants, and even minerals. Some healers claim that the aura changes color according to moods, or because of sickness. Rose Gladden believed that this change in color was not because of illness. She said the color changed when a person's aura was out of balance. This was what caused a person to become sick.

ANCIENT AURAS

The idea of the aura is very old. It appears in the art and writings of ancient Egypt, Greece, Rome, and India. In the 16th century, the Swiss doctor Philippus Aureolus Paracelsus described it as a round, "fiery" object. The 18th-century Swedish scientist and psychic Emanuel Swedenborg said it surrounded everyone.

This is a picture of Philippus Aureolus Paracelsus. In the 16th century he described what an aura looked like.

In the 1840s Baron Karl von Reichenbach, a German scientist, did an experiment. He asked some people to sit in a dark room. They claimed to have psychic powers. Then Von Reichenbach showed them various living things and objects. They said they saw flamelike energy shooting out from animals, plants, magnets, and certain crystals. Von Reichenbach called this energy "odic force."

In 1911 Walter J. Kilner was a doctor at St. Thomas's Hospital, London. He found a way for scientists to see an

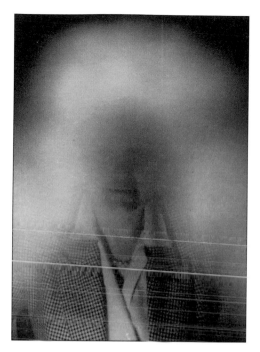

This photograph shows a greenish-yellow aura. Some doctors claim that a patient's aura can tell them what is wrong with the patient.

aura. He looked at the human body through a special blue-colored liquid called dicyanin. Later, it was discovered that a type of glass that was made in the former Czechoslovakia could be used in the same way. Because of the deep blue color of the liquid, the glowing aura showed up as a faint blue-gray cloud against a black background. It surrounded the human body. It could also be seen around magnets.

A few years later, Dr. Kilner worked out a way to diagnose sickness from people's auras. His ideas, however, were not taken seriously at the time. Nevertheless, by the time of his death in 1920, other people were starting to take an interest in his work.

PROOF ON FILM

In 1939 a Russian scientist, Semyon Davidovich Kirlian, did some experiments. He took photographs of what seemed to be a kind of aura. The idea was not new. As early as 1898, another Russian, Yakov Narkevich-Todko, had put similar pictures on show at an exhibition of his work.

Kirlian took pictures of his own hand for his first experiments. He put his hand on a special piece of film inside a dark box. Then he took the photograph. It showed a strange glow coming from his fingertips. With his wife, Valentina, also a scientist, Kirlian went

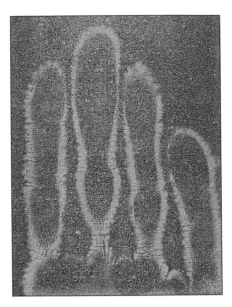

Semyon Davidovich Kirlian photographed his own aura in 1939. However, what became known as "Kirlian" photographs were not new. The picture above was taken in 1898. It shows the aura of a girl said to have been suffering from anemia, or lack of red blood cells in the bloodstream.

on to take pictures of many living things and different objects. Their first pictures were taken on black and white film. Later they worked in color.

THE RESULTS

It is said that Kirlian's pictures were able to reveal changes in the mood and health of a person. The colors, patterns of light, and brightness of the aura appeared to change if a person was happy or sad, or if a person was in good health or sick.

In the 1970s, Thelma Moss and Kendall Johnson carried out some experiments at the University of California's Center for Health Studies in Los Angeles. They also used pictures to show auras. They were surprised to find that a plant's glowing aura changed when a human hand touched it. When part of a leaf was cut off, a glowing outline of the missing piece could still be seen on the picture.

In Russia, Viktor Adamenko found that in humans the brightest glows were given off at points relating to those used by acupuncturists. This seemed to give a connection between the life force *chi*, and a person's aura. Some healers are excited by these "Kirlian" photographs. They say they prove that auras exist.

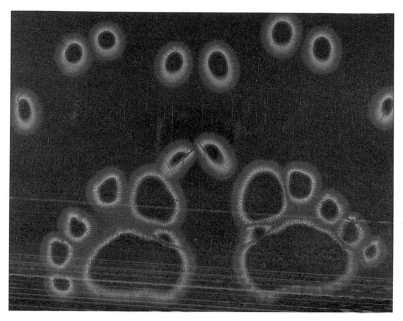

This is a "Kirlian" photograph of a person's fingertips and toes. The person was a patient of German healer Peter Mandel, who took the picture.

ALL IN THE EYES

Another way of "seeing" illness is to look at the iris, which is the colored part of the eye. This is called "iridology." Doctors have known for a long time that the eyes of a patient can show if he or she is ill. However, it was only in the mid-19th century that iridology was recognized as a science.

Around 160 years ago, there was a boy in Hungary named Ignatz Peczely. He kept a pet owl. Owls have very large eyes. When his owl was injured, Ignatz noticed that a mark suddenly appeared on its iris.

Years later, Peczely became a doctor. He remembered his pet owl. He wondered if human eyes also changed when a person was ill. While he was working in a hospital in Budapest, Peczely began to study the question. He kept notes of what the irises of his patients looked like before he started to treat them.

The colored iris is round. Peczely drew diagrams, or maps, of his patients' eyes. He marked any changes he found on these diagrams. He discovered that every illness seemed to cause marks in different parts of the iris. When the patients became well again, the marks faded, or even disappeared.

Each area of the iris map is said to be related to a particular part . . . of the body.

HOW IRIDOLOGY WORKS

Doctors in Europe became interested in Dr. Peczely's results. Then, early in the 20th century, iridology was introduced to the U.S. by Dr. Nils Liljequist, the Swedish healer. In the 1950s, an American doctor, Dr. Bernard Jensen, drew up a map of the iris. This is the one that is still used today by iridologists. The iris is divided into pieces, like slices of a pie. There are more than 40 "pie slices," and some are also divided into other smaller sections. In total, there are 96 areas in the iris that are used in diagnosis.

Human eye colors are usually blue, brown, or gray. They are sometimes mixed colors such as green or brown-green. The marks on the iris can be orange, yellow, red, green, or white—or often they are just very dark. Sometimes the same marks can be seen in both eyes but in the opposite position.

Each area of the iris map is said to be related to a particular part or area of the body, for example, to the lungs or kidneys. There are also areas related to the flow of blood through the body and to the nerves.

Fine white marks in the iris are said to be the result of stress, or extreme worry caused by the problems of life. Dark patches are caused by lack of energy. Dark, fuzzy rings around the outside of the iris are said to be because of a buildup of poisons in the blood. This can happen if a person drinks too much coffee, tea, or alcohol. It also happens to heavy smokers.

EARLY WARNING SIGNALS

Iridologists believe that any illness in a person shows up on the iris long before a doctor is able to find it by other means. They say that this makes iridology an important way of making an early diagnosis of serious disease. This could mean the difference between life and death for the patient.

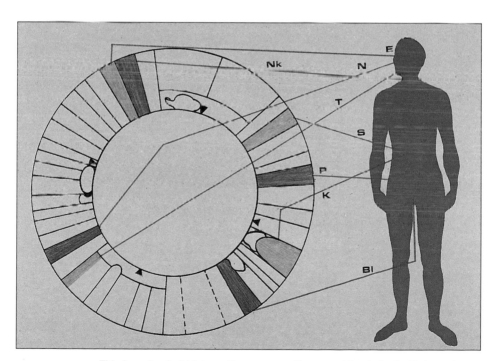

This is a simple iridology diagram sometimes used by students. It shows how some parts of the iris relate to different parts of the body. E = ear; Nk = neck; S = spleen; K = kidney; N = nose; T = tonsils; Bl = bladder; P = posterior.

Scientific Tests

Many scientists refuse to believe in psychic healing. Some, however, have tried to find an explanation for it.

In 1957 a man named Bernard Grad met a Hungarian named Oskar Estabany. Grad was a scientist at McGill University in Montreal, Canada. Estabany claimed to be a healer.

Grad asked Estabany to take part in an experiment. This involved plants. Some seeds were planted in different pots. They were kept very dry. Usually plants would not grow well under such conditions. Grad wanted to see if Estabany could "cure" them. Estabany was given a jar of slightly salty water. He held it in his hands for 15 minutes each day. Later, the seeds were watered by a scientist. One group of seeds was watered with Estabany's salty water. The other group was watered from a jar of salty water that Estabany had not touched.

GROWING POWER

After 14 days Grad checked the seeds. He counted the seeds that had started to grow. This was the same in both groups. Then he measured the height of the seedlings, or young plants that have been grown from seeds. Those that had been watered from Estabany's jar were much taller than those in the other group.

These plant seedlings (opposite) are being grown in a science laboratory. Bernard Grad used plants like these to test the powers of the psychic healer Oskar Estabany.

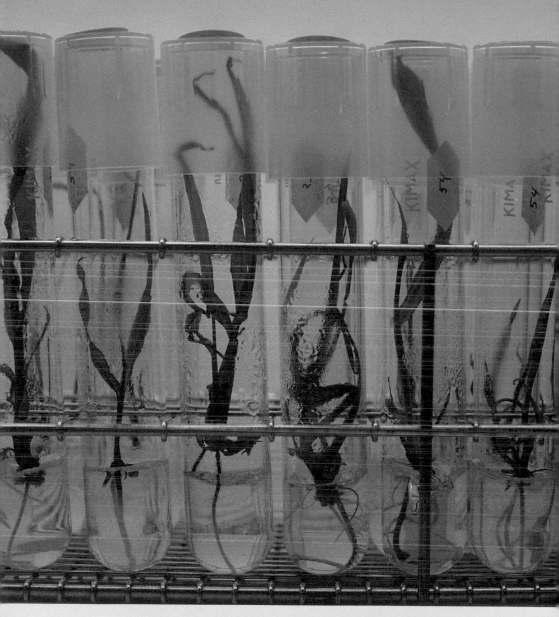

. . . he measured the height of the seedlings. Those that had been watered from Estabany's jar were much taller . . .

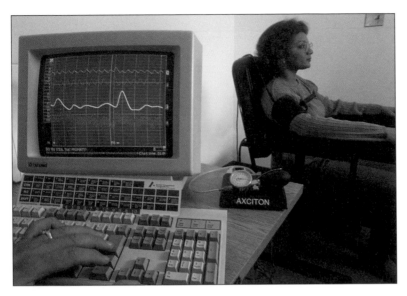

This is a computerized polygraph, or lie detector, machine. A blood pressure-pulse cuff is strapped around the arm of the person being tested and a tube is fastened around the chest. Changes in the person's blood pressure and pulse are recorded on the computer screen. Dr. Braud's tests in Texas were done on a machine something like this.

THE HUMAN TOUCH

At the Mind Science Foundation in San Antonio, Texas, Dr. William Braud decided to try tests something like this on humans, rather than plants.

Braud set up an experiment that was designed to work as well as possible. He didn't want any possibility of mistakes. The equipment he used was very similar to something called a polygraph machine, or lie detector. A lie detector works by noting all the changes in a person's breathing, blood pressure, or pulse. If a person is asked a question and answers it with a lie, he or she is likely to sweat, the pulse may be faster, and the blood pressure may increase. The lie detector notes these changes. The person carrying out the test can then see that the answer to the question was probably a lie.

Dr. Braud found a group of 32 people who were suffering from headaches, high blood pressure, or stress. He first divided them into two groups of 16. He then tested them with his machine. One group, called the "active" group, showed a change when they were put in a stressful situation. The others, the "inactive" group, did not.

Each person was then tested separately. One at a time, they sat in a room and were told to relax. Braud and another scientist, Marilyn Schlitz, sat in a different room. In front of them was a screen that showed the readings from the machine.

Manning was able to alter Lorenz's brain patterns using the power of his mind.

Braud and Schlitz took turns at trying to change the readings. They tried a type of telepathy, using the power of their minds to make the person calm down. The people in the "inactive" group showed no changes. But the readings from the "active" group changed completely. Somehow the scientists had been able to calm them down!

AMAZING RESULTS

In 1977 Matthew Manning was just 21 years old. It was claimed then that he had psychokinetic powers. Psychokinetic means "able to move or change things using only the power of the mind." Several scientists wanted to know if Manning could use his powers to change or affect another person's brain waves.

Manning went to the University of California at Davis to take part in some tests. In one test, Manning and Professor Fred Lorenz were linked to an electro-encephalograph (EEG). This is a machine that records brain activity. Manning was able to alter Lorenz's brain patterns by using the power of his mind.

Other scientists did more tests on Manning at the Science Unlimited Research Foundation in San Antonio, Texas. It was claimed that he had the power to destroy cancer cells. Some said that he had scored successes in 27 out of 30 cases.

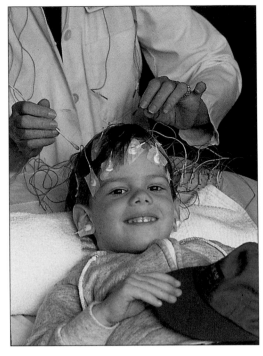

This boy is about to have his brain waves recorded by an electroencephalograph. In 1977 Matthew Manning and Fred Lorenz were linked to a machine like this. It was part of a scientific test to see if it was possible to alter brain patterns using psychokinetic powers.

MORE TESTS

Manning took part in other tests at Birkbeck College, London University. Professor John Hasted gave him a sample of an enzyme. An enzyme is one of a huge group of chemicals that control how the human body works. The enzyme in Hasted's test was called *monoamine oxidase*. If this enzyme is not working properly it can be one of the causes of migraines, or very bad headaches. Manning thought hard about the enzyme sample, then Hasted examined it. He said that its makeup had changed. However, other scientists refused to believe that this was true.

SCIENTIFIC OPINION

So how do scientists and doctors feel about the different kinds of healing described in this book? Many refuse to believe in any of them—although numerous patients claim to have been cured.

Some scientists who claim not to believe in the powers of healing think that such "cures" are all in the mind of the patient. Because patients want to feel better, they become better. However, this is in fact how many healers achieve their results. It is the power of the mind over the illness.

ILLNESSES CAUSED BY THE MIND

In recent years doctors have begun to agree that there are such things as "psychosomatic" illnesses. *Psychosomatic* is formed from two Greek words, meaning "mind" and "body." Although nobody really understands how it happens, it is thought that a number of illnesses seem to be caused—or at least are directly affected by the state of the mind. In particular, certain skin conditions are known to become worse when the patient is suffering from stress or worry.

Perhaps the use of psychic healing is related to other powers of the mind. One example is telepathy (the transmitting or sending of "messages" from one mind to another). People

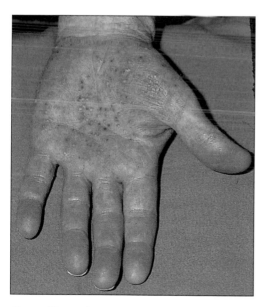

Some skin conditions, such as the rash on this man's hand, are thought to be caused by stress or worry. This is called a psychosomatic illness.

45

Matthew Manning, the world-famous psychic healer. Despite doing many scientific tests on him, scientists have been unable to explain his powers.

who are telepathic often describe feeling a current of energy flowing from them. This might explain the current of energy that most healers say seems to flow between them and their patients. However, although it is possible that a telepathic "message" could be sent to animals, it does not explain how plants could be affected. Plants have no brain.

LIVING PROOF

Many healers believe they are drawing on some powerful energy that is unknown to science. How this energy can flow through their hands, or be sent over distances, is unexplained. But healers certainly seem to become exhausted after healing a patient.

Despite the disbelief of so many scientists and doctors, there are some people still living who would otherwise have died. Thousands of people all over the world stand by their belief in psychic healing.

Glossary

ancestor A member of the same family from a previous generation.

channel Something through which something else, such as water, information, or energy, flows. Also to direct toward a particular purpose.

circulation The flow of blood around the body. Also moving around freely.

conventional Traditional, or following commonly accepted beliefs and standards.

electroencephalograph (EEG) A machine that detects and records the pattern of brain waves.

function The special task or purpose of a machine, person, or part of the human body.

hypnotist A person who puts others into sleeplike states.

investigators People who carry out in-depth studies of a subject in order to find out the truth.

iridology The study of the iris (the colored part of the eye) in order to determine a person's state of health. A person who carries out such studies is an iridologist.

life forces The mysterious energy that sustains all human life. In Far Eastern countries, everything in the universe is made up of the life forces of yin and yang.

miracles Amazing events that are impossible to explain according to any known laws of nature.

posterior At the rear, or buttocks.

psychic A person who has unexplained powers of the mind.

psychokinetic Moving or altering the appearance or behavior of something using only the power of the mind.

qualified Someone who has been trained in a particular subject, and who has a certificate to prove it.

spiritual Of or relating to feelings or emotions, rather than to the body or other physical matters.

spiritualism A belief in various otherwordly, or spiritual, powers.

stethoscope A medical instrument used for listening to sounds made inside the body.

stress Extreme worry caused by the various problems of daily life.

surgeons Doctors who specialize in different forms of surgery.

telepathy Mind reading, or the sending of thoughts from one person's mind to another.

yoga A Hindu practice teaching control of the mind and body in order to achieve physical and spiritual health.

Index

Further Reading

Brownstone, David M., and Irene M. Franck. *Healers*, "Work Throughout History" series. Facts on File, 1989
Burgess, John. *Psychic and Spirit Phenomena: Believers and Skeptics*, P.P.I Publishing, Kettering, OH, 1991
Gordon, James S. *Holistic Medicine*, "Encyclopedia of Health" series. Chelsea House, 1988
Stewart, Gail B. *Alternative Healing: Opposing Viewpoints*, "Great Mysteries" series. Greenhaven, 1990